Cancún

The Delaplaine
2020 Long Weekend Guide

Andrew Delaplaine

NO BUSINESS HAS PAID A SINGLE PENNY OR GIVEN _ANYTHING_ TO BE INCLUDED IN THIS BOOK.

Senior Editors
Renee & Sophie Delaplaine
Copyright Gramercy Park Press

Gramercy Park Press
New York London Paris

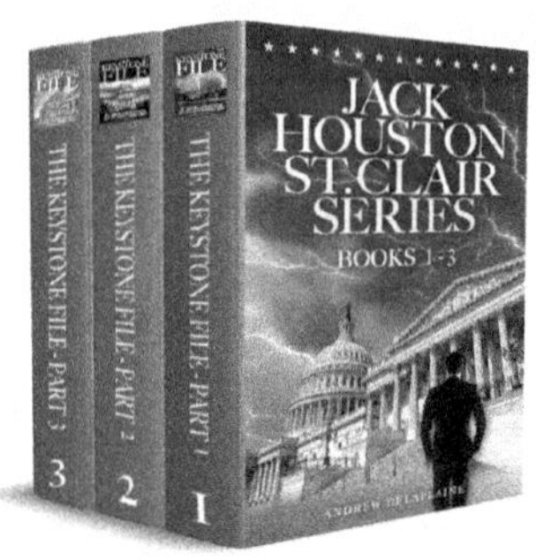

WANT 3 **FREE** THRILLERS?

Why, of course you do!

If you like these writers--
Vince Flynn, Brad Thor, Tom Clancy, James Patterson, David Baldacci, John Grisham, Brad Meltzer, Daniel Silva, Don DeLillo
If you like these TV series –
House of Cards, Scandal, West Wing, The Good Wife, Madam Secretary, Designated Survivor

You'll love the **unputdownable** series about Jack Houston St. Clair, with political intrigue, romance, and loads of action and suspense.

Besides writing travel books, I've written political thrillers for many years that have delighted hundreds of thousands of readers. I want to introduce you to my work!
Send me an email and I'll send you a link where you can download the first 3 books in my bestselling series, **absolutely FREE.**

Mention **this book** when you email me.

andrewdelaplaine@mac.com

The Delaplaine
Long Weekend Guide

TABLE OF CONTENTS

Chapter 1
FIRST THINGS FIRST

Why Cancún?

Being world travelers, we knew the reputation of Cancún. We knew that Cancún is the Mecca of spring breakers and pasty Americans desperately seeking a weekend respite from biting winters. So it was with trepidation that, years ago, we first stepped foot on that hotel-covered sandbar. We dutifully wiggled into our bathing suits, slathered ourselves in sunblock, and walked out onto the beach. And then we finally understood it – we got why millions of people every year flock to this far corner of the Yucatán Peninsula. *Cancún has got a world-class beach.*

We have been on many beaches around the world. And none of them are quite as magical as the one in Cancún. The sun is strong, but a constant gentle breeze keeps one comfortable. On first sight, you will not believe the color of the water you're looking at actually exists in nature. It really is a clear, bright turquoise. Waves lap gently on fine sand the color of cappuccino. The slope is very gradual, so you can head far into the water and still touch the bottom. And the temperature of the water is perfect year-round.

But there is more. There is something else about this beach that we just can't put our finger on. There is an idyllic serenity the likes of which we have never encountered before or since. Here we find an eclectic mix of all kinds, local and tourist. Here we find an elderly couple holding hands staring at the sea, a few yards from a group of beer-chugging frat boys. And all the people have a blissed-out, faraway smile on their faces. Yes, there is something magical about the beach in Cancún.

Mind you, Cancún is a tourist town. By far, the local industry is tourism, and most of what goes on in Cancún is designed to separate you from what you have in your wallet. If you are looking to get to know the culture and people the Yucatán Peninsula, Cancún is not the place for you. It is for good reason that Yucatecans call Cancún "Gringolandia." If you want to experience the true culture of the area, you will have to go to the ancient city of nearby Mérida.

Transportation & Tips for Getting Around

AIRPORT & TAXIS

Cancún Airport can be an unnerving and high-pressure experience. As soon as you disembark, you'll encounter dozens of pushy vendors representing various businesses, all trying to sell you (and sell you *hard*) a timeshare or a tour, or even just a taxi ride. The taxi people and cabbies can be very pushy. Take my advice and do yourself a favor—book yourself a pickup service before you arrive. They will meet you as you arrive and usher you through the craziness to your waiting van. You'll be at your hotel before you know it. (Many hotels offer free transfers—check to be sure.)

Rates from the airport run up to $60 one way, 20-mile trip to the Zona Hotelera (Hotel Zone). They only charge you half when you go the other way.

SHUTTLE SERVICE

A cheaper shuttle service is operated by Hertz and the Green Line. It runs every half hour. Buy your ticket when you get here.

BUS SERVICE

There's bus service from the airport into Cancun that runs just a few dollars.

RENTING A CAR

Renting a car is a great way to explore the many opportunities the Yucatán Peninsula has to offer. I recommend reserving your car ahead of time. When renting your car, it is **very important** that you specifically request insurance equal to the value of the car. It is not made clear when you pick it up, but you are personally responsible for any damage to the car. Upon return you are at the mercy of the staff for any scratch, so be very aware of the condition of the vehicle when you get it and make sure each ding and dent is noted in the rental agreement before you drive away. It's better to arrange your rental before you leave on your trip to be assured you get a car. All the major car rental firms are represented here.

CANCUN MUNICIPAL TOURISM OFFICE
Corner of Avenida Nader & Avenida Cobá: 998-887-3379. Open weekdays.

CANCUN CONVENTION BUREAU
www.cancun.travel (no .com after travel)

GENERAL INFORMATION
www.cancun.com
www.cancuntips.com

HOTEL

Chapter 2
LODGINGS

Timeshares

Budget - Cuidad Cancun (Downtown)

Budget - Isla Cancun (Beach-Zona Hotelera)
Moderate – Isla Cancun (Beach-Zona Hotelera)
Luxury – Isla Cancun (Beach-Zona Hotelera)

TIMESHARES

A word about timeshares. Many hotels and resorts in
Cancún are associated with timeshare programs.
Visitors are often invited to a timeshare presentation

in return for a complimentary gift, such as a free meal. We urge you to attend the presentation ONLY IF YOU ARE SINCERELY INTERESTED IN A TIMESHARE. We have been to more timeshare presentations than we care to think about and we can assure you the complimentary gift is never worth the inconvenience. Sales techniques are tricky and often high-pressure, and more than one innocent vacationer has awakened the next day with a bad case of buyer's remorse. So if you are approached with a timeshare invitation, we urge you to firmly say NO and walk away. These people (they're under a lot of pressure themselves because they only get paid after they fleece you) do not give a damn about you, and you can't—*repeat, CAN'T*—hurt their feelings. So do not give them the time of day.

Budget - Cuidad Cancun (Downtown)

SOL Y LUNA
Calle Alcatraces 33, Parque Las Palapas, Lote 33 Mz. 9 SM 22, Quintana Roo,
Cancun: 52-998-887-5579
http://caribya.com/cancun/sol.y.luna/
 Situated on the floors above a tapas place you'll find this 10-room inn. Nothing fancy, but basic and nice. Perfect for exploring downtown where most of the locals live. A nice enough little eatery is located on premises, El Rincón del Vino.

XBALAMQUÉ

Av. Yaxchilán 31, Sm. 22, Mz. 17, Quintana Roo,
Cancun: 52-998-193-2720
www.xbalamque.com
This place is a real find. The furnishings are very
much reflective of the countryside, with great tile-
work. They've tried to make the whole place look
very Mayan, with yard after yard of murals, paintings
and sculptures done in that style. All the furniture is
very rough-hewn (but you'll wish you had a few
pieces when you get back home.) There's a
refreshingly calming waterfall in the pool area.
There's a beautifully quaint courtyard and they have a
few junior suites. (Food in the Adelita restaurant is
good, too, and those cool local beers are great.)

GRAND ROYAL LAGOON

Calle Quetzal No. 8-A | Boulevard Kukulcán Km 7.5, 52-998-883-2749
https://bighotels.org/product/grand-royal-lagoon/
If you want to stay in the Hotel Zone on a budget, then this is the place for you. It is interestingly located on the back side of the sandbar on the lagoon, so don't expect to walk out your door onto the beach. But the beach is in walking distance, and all beachfront is common property in Mexico, so feel free to use another hotel's beach. It is also a short walk to shopping and the big clubs the zone is known for. The rooms are basic and clean; the showers are big with plenty of hot water and good pressure. Most rooms have kitchenettes. We recommend upgrading to a balcony for $10. The breakfast is tasty.

HOTEL DEL SOL

Av. Lopez Portillo Mz 2Lt 1A SM85, Puerto Juarez, Mexico: 52-998-880-3693
www.hotel-del-sol.cancunhotelmexico.net/en
This hotel is not in Cancún proper, it is in Puerto Juarez, about eight kilometers north of Cancún, so it is a bit far from the all the attractions of the city and the Hotel/Beach Zone. It is, however, perfectly located forsea ad excursions to Isla de Mujeres, with the ferry right across the street. The hotel has excellent views of the ocean, but there is no serviceable beach for miles, and there is no pool. The rooms are very clean and the service efficient.

HOTEL EL REY DEL CARIBE

Av. Uxmal 24 | Corner of Uxmal and
Nader, Cancún 77500, Mexico:
52-998-884-2028
www.reycaribe.com
This lovely hotel can be appropriately described as an
oasis. It is located in downtown Cancún, but once
you've entered the compound you feel as though
you've entered another world. The gardens are
simply wonderful. You'll enjoy the hammocks by the
pool. This is an eco-conscious hotel, so you'll
appreciate all the green touches. The rooms are big,
and on the upper floors include a kitchenette.

HOTEL RAMADA CANCÚN CITY

Avenida Yaxchilan 41, Cancún 77500, Mexico: 52-
998-881-7870/ 800-640-7473
www.ramadacancun.com
Another good, clean basic hotel. It is located in the
city proper, but they have a free shuttle to the Beach
/Hotel Zone. There are a lot of good restaurants in
the area, but also consider the hotel restaurant; it is

surprisingly good. The staff is courteous and professional.

TERRACARIBE HOTEL
Av Lopez Portillo 70 | Esquina Av. Bonampak, Cancún 77500, Mexico: 52 998 211 3015, 1-800-837-7222 https://terracaribehotelboutique.com-cancun.com/ This place likes to bill itself as a boutique hotel. It's not a boutique hotel, it's just a plain no-frills hotel. But it is a clean hotel with good service. The staff here are very friendly. The downside is the location, it is in the city and the neighborhood is a little rustic. The restaurant food is tasty, and the bar offers good drinks and great service. All in all, a great value.

SOTAVENTO HOTEL AND YACHT CLUB
Blv. Kukulkan km 4 Zona Hotelera | Lote D.8.3 Calle Pescador, Cancún 77500, Mexico: 52-998-884-1540 http://www.hotelsotavento.info/ Located on the northern edge of the Beach/Hotel Zone across the street from the beach hotels, and overlooking the lagoon. It is a basic no frills hotel with a nice pool and garden area.

SUITES GABY HOTEL
Av. Sunyaxche Lote 46 y 47 | Mza 2 Supermanzana 25 CP, Cancún 77509, Mexico: 52-998-887-8037 https://www.suitesgaby.com.mx/index A decent basic hotel in the center of Cancún. The rooms are clean with internet available. It is conveniently located near the bus station and also quite close to the tourist market.

ALL RITMO RESORT & WATERPARK
Km 1.5 Carretera a Punta Juarez-Punta
Sam, Cancún 77500, Mexico: 52 81 5350 3400/ 877-
734-3186
www.allritmocancun.com
 As you can tell from the name, this is a very kid-
friendly resort. But it is also lots of fun for adults.
The staff is very keyed in to entertaining and offering
a good time. There are all sorts of activities offered,
such as the waterpark, games, snorkeling, boating and
surprisingly good Vegas-style shows in the evening.
The rooms are very large and well maintained. The
hotel is located off the tourist strip, up north a bit in
Puerto Juarez, and is conveniently located near the
ferry to Isla Mujeres.

AVALON BACCARA

Blvd. Kukulcan Km 11.5 | Zona
Hotelera, Cancún 77500, Mexico:
998-881-3900/ 1-800-507-1239
www.hotelavalonbaccaracancun.com
The Avalon Baccara, is, put simply, an excellent
hotel. It is quiet and intimate. There are only about
30 rooms in the hotel. The setting is peaceful and out
of the way. The staff, from the management to the
maids, is consistent in the superior service they offer.
The rooms are spotless and relaxing, each one
featuring a balcony with Jacuzzi. The grounds are
well-kept, from the colorful pool to the groomed
beach. The food is delicious. We can't recommend
enough the Avalon Baccara.

BEL AIR COLLECTION RESORT & SPA

Boulevard Kukulcan Km. 20.5 Hotel
Zone, Cancún 77500, Mexico:
52-800-400-2040/01 800 523 2223
www.belaircancun.com
There is good and bad at the Bel Air. Let's get the
bad out of the way. The building is old and it has old
building problems. Air conditioning problems is a
constant battle for the maintenance staff. Now the
good -- the staff is very efficient and courteous. The
common areas are comfortable and stylish. Most of
the common areas are open air and accented by
billowing white curtains. The food is quite good,
particularly the Italian restaurant, Ciao Mexico.   We
also recommend the spa… a massage on the beach in

the evening is just the thing before hitting the nightclubs or puttering off to bed.

KRYSTAL GRAND PUNTA CANCUN

Blvd Kukulcan Km 8.5, Hotel Zone, Cancún 77500, Mexico:
998-891-5555
www.krystal-hotels.com
The building is a bit dated, but is well-maintained. The lobby tends to get a bit warm, but the rooms have excellent AC. The hotel is tall, so the upper floors have excellent views no matter what side you are one. Location is everything, and the Krystal has excellent location. The hotel sits in a quiet cul-de-sac just next to the nightclub zone and restaurants. It also boasts one of the best sections of beach, where the water is most calm.

LE BLANC SPA

Blvd. Kukulkan Km. 10, Cancún, 888-702-0913
www.leblancsparesort.com
An adults-only beach all-inclusive resort offers 260 rooms with balconies featuring great ocean or lagoon views – many with sitting areas and whirlpool tubs. Amenities include: flat-screen LED TVs, Bvlgari bath amenities, 24-hour butler services, complimentary Wi-Fi, complimentary breakfast and parking. Hotel facilities include: 4 on-site dining options, 6 bars, fitness center, golf course, outdoor pools, and the **Blanc Spa** (with those long white curtains billowing in the breeze, just like in the movies). Beach access. AAA Five Diamond Award.

MARRIOTT CASAMAGNA CANCÚN RESORT

Blvd Kukulcan, Retorno Chac L-41 | Zona
Hotelera, Cancún 77500, Mexico: 52-998-881-2000
www.marriott.com
The Marriott offers everything you would expect
from a resort hotel. Room service is quick. The
rooms are large and clean. We recommend you
spring for an ocean view. Also, when booking your
room, get the package that includes the breakfast
buffet. Trust us, you'll be glad you did. The
CasaMagna breakfast buffet is the stuff of legends.

NIZUC RESORT & SPA

Blvd Kukulkan Mz 59 Lote 1-01 Km 21.26, Cancun,
+52 998 891 5700
www.nizuc.com
An ideal resort for golf lovers, beachfront resort is
located right next to a golf course. Though this is a
large resort (about 30 acres), it feels much more
intimate because of the mangroves surrounding the
place. There's a barrier reef not far from the shore, so
explore that when you go snorkeling. This resort
offers 274 soundproofed rooms with high ceilings.
The garden villas offer more privacy, if that's what
you're looking for. The penthouse suites have
"outdoor living rooms." Amenities include:
complimentary Wi-Fi, iPod docks, flat-screen TVs,
Nespresso machines and minibars. Resort facilities
include: 6 restaurants (including **Terra Nostra**, with
an Italian motif and the modern Mexican spot
Ramona), 2 lounge bars, 2 pools, tennis courts, a
full-service spa, and a gym. Family friendly facility.

Conveniently located near attractions like the Playa Delfines beach and the Interactive Aquarium.

OMNI CANCÚN HOTEL
Blvd Kukulcan km 16.5, Hotel
Zone, Cancún 77500, Mexico: 52-998-881-0600
www.omnihotels.com
The Omni is still a good hotel, but it may be a bit on the old side. The beds are very comfortable, but the rooms are small and the bathrooms are smaller.
You'll get great service from the staff, particularly the beach staff. The food is not very impressive, so head out when dining.

TEMPTATION RESORT SPA CANCÚN
Blvd. Kukulcan km 3.5 | Zona Hotelera/ Hotel
Zone, Cancún 77500, Mexico: 52-998-848-7900/
877-485-8367
https://www.temptation-experience.com/
Temptation is an all-inclusive adults-only resort, which means you can eat and/or drink to your heart's content, and you can probably find someone to do it with you. There is a definite party atmosphere.

There are lots of ways to meet people, with activities going on round the clock. It has a reputation as a bit of a swingers' hotel. But you don't have to be a horny single to enjoy the resort. There is a "sexy" pool and there is a "quiet" pool. Rooms are clean, staff is on the ball, and the food is pretty good. We recommend The Wok restaurant.

WESTIN LAGUNAMAR CANCÚN

Km 12.5 Blvd Kukulcan | Zona Hotelera, PO Box 834 Apdo., Cancún 77500, Mexico: 52-998-891-4200
www.marriott.com/hotels
This is a timeshare resort. They are going to want you to listen to their sales pitch, which we recommend you avoid unless you really are interested. The hotel facilities are top notch. All the suites have wifi, balconies, washer/dryers, and kitchens stocked with some basics. If cooking your own food is not your idea of a vacation, the hotel is in walking distance of some very excellent restaurants, which the hotel staff will happily direct you to. They will also help you with the myriad of activities offered at the resort. The grounds are beautiful, and their pool and fountain system is spectacular.

Luxury – Isla Cancun (Beach-Zona Hotelera)

EXCELLENCE RIVIERA

Carretera Federal 307 Chetumal, Puerto Juarez | Manzana 7, Lote 1, S.M. 11, Puerto Morelos 77580, Mexico: 52-998-872-8500, 1-866-540-2585
www.excellence-resorts.com

The Excellence is an all-inclusive resort located in Puerto Morelos, just south of Cancún. The staff really stresses the notion that you are home. That is if your home has hundreds of servants running around anticipating your every wish. And should your wish be a drink, then you are in the right spot. The bar staff is very knowledgeable, and they serve only quality brands. If you don't care for alcohol, we highly recommend the cucumber lemonade. Foodwise there are 8 on site restaurants to choose from. We recommend the tepanyaki. Room service is quick and available 24 hours a day.

FIESTA AMERICANA GRAND CORAL BEACH RESORT & SPA

Blvd Kukulcan Km 9.5 Lote 6 | Zona
Hotelera, Cancún 77500, Mexico:
998-881-3200, 1-800-343-7821
www.fiestamericanagrand.com
Just what you'd expect from a five star hotel. The staff is courteous and always there with anything you need. The rooms are well-designed. Beds are luxurious with lots of comfy pillows. The bathrooms are almost entire suites in themselves. The food in the restaurants is pricey, but well worth it. Despite the name, this is not a party hotel – things quiet down after midnight, but it is within stumbling distance of the nightclubs, if that's your thing.

RITZ-CARLTON

Retorno del Rey 36 | Zona Hotelera, Quintana
Roo, Cancún 77500, Mexico: 52-998-881-0808
www.ritzcarlton.com

As one would expect from the Ritz-Carlton, this is a sumptuously laid out resort. The building and the grounds are beautiful. All that can be said of the rooms is they are perfect. The pool areas are luxurious and relaxing. The staff is always on the lookout for a way to make you more comfortable. The fitness area features state of the art equipment, and there is bottled water and fresh towels at every station. The beach, of course, is beautiful, relaxing and perfectly groomed. If you plan on using a cabana at the beach, reserve it ahead of time. Upgrading to the hotel's Club Level will get you ever more stellar services and luxury, and all food, drinks and alcohol are included. If you are a fan of the Ritz's exceptional food, which can be quite pricey, you can save considerably by upgrading.

RIU PALACE LAS AMERICAS
Blvd Kukulcan, Km 8.5, Manzana 50 | Lote 4, Zona Hotelera, Cancún 77500, Mexico: 52-998-891-4300/ 888-666-8816
www.riu.com

All-inclusive resort on the Hotel-zone. The staff is friendly. The building is a bit old, and by today's standards, the rooms are small. Also, the walls are rather thin, and you had better hope for a quiet neighbor. That said, the staff is working constantly to keep the grounds in good condition. The food is pretty good, and there's lots of top-shelf booze. 24 hour room service is also a nice touch.

LIVE AQUA ALL-INCLUSIVE
Boulevard Kukulcan Km. 12.5 Zona
Hotelera, Cancún 77500, Mexico: 52-998-881-7600/
800-343-7821
www.feel-aqua.com
The building here is very beautiful and well designed, there is a light and airy feel to the place. Walking in to the lobby for the first time is an impressive sight. The pools are ubiquitous; you could swim in a different pool every day, and still not hit them all in a week. And in that week you will never see or hear a

child… they are simply not allowed. The rooms are nice … great if you upgrade to a suite. The staff is friendly. Drinks can be a bit weak, so feel free to order an extra shot. We found the food at Live Aqua to be a bit weak also. Of the restaurant options, the best is MB.

MOON PALACE GOLF & SPA RESORT
Carretera Federal 307 Km
340, Cancún 77500, Mexico: 52-998-881-6000/ 800-986-5632
www.moonpalacecancun.com
All-inclusive. The resort is huge, so take advantage of the many golf carts. All rooms have a balcony. Obviously one of the big draws of this place are the golf courses, which have been installed with a respect for the local environment, so while you're teeing off, you might get a chance to see a crocodile.

SUN PALACE
Blvd. Kukulcan KM. 20 | Zona
Hotelera, Cancún 77500, Mexico: 800-986-5632
www.palaceresorts.com
Devoted guests tend to come back to the Sun Palace year after year. The staff is warm and friendly and very accommodating. We recommend you upgrade to the concierge level; the extra amenities and superior room make it well worth it. All the rooms in the hotel are large and comfortable. Our only issue is the toilets in the bathrooms could stand to have some privacy walls if you are going to be sharing the bathroom.

ZOETRY PARAISO DE LA BONITA

Carretera Cancún-Chetumal km 328, Puerto
Morelos 77580, Mexico: 52-998-872-8300
www.zoetryresorts.com
The Zoetry is not actually in Cancún, but in Puerto
Morelos, a few minutes south, but is about the same
distance from the airport. Speaking of airport, one
very nice feature is the hotel will pick you up, so you
don't have to worry about taxis. Being away from the
tourist zone of Cancún, the resort feels secluded and
peaceful. When you get to your room you'll find a
bottle of champagne and a bottle of tequila… live it
up. The food here is healthy and delicious, with many
dishes featuring organic ingredients.

THE ROYAL CANCÚN

Kukulkan Km 11.5 Hotel
Kukulcan Km. 4.5 Lotes C2 & C2A, Zona Hotelera,
77500 Cancún, QROO, Mexico, 52 800 888 7744
www.royalresorts.com

This is an excellent all-inclusive resort and the flagship of Real Resorts. First class service through and through. The rooms are fantastic. Finicky sleepers will love the beds and appreciate the "Pillow Menu." Each room has dispensers of call-brand whiskey, vodka, rum and tequila. You are never at a want for anything. There is a variety of different restaurants in the hotel, most notable is the Asiana. The hotel buffet is a little ho-hum. The beach is always impeccably groomed. And for those of you who can't stand to be out of touch, there is a strong wifi signal everywhere.

Chapter 3
RESTAURANTS

Budget

100% NATURAL
Juices, Sandwiches, Lunch, Healthy, Vegetarian, Vegan
Av. Sunyaxche lote 62, Supermanzana 25, Mza. 6
(Col. Centro), Cancún, Quintana Roo 77500, Mexico:
52-998-884-0102
www.100natural.com.mx
100% Natural is a restaurant chain that is happily
taking Mexico by storm. The food offered is free of

preservatives and artificial flavors and colorings. For breakfast, lunch and dinner, healthy fare is the theme. The juice bar offers fresh made juices from local fruits and veggies. The delicious whole-wheat bread is baked fresh on-site, so try one of their tasty sandwiches. We recommend the veggie burger.

CALYPSO'S GRILL AND MEXICAN FOOD
Seafood, Mexican
Kukulcan Ave. km 8.5 next to Cancun
Center, Cancún 77500, Mexico:
52 998-883-1244 / 52 998-214-5393
www.calypsoscancunrestaurant.com
WEBSITE DOWN AT PRESSTIME
Calypso's is a good basic no-frills restaurant in the Hotel Zone across from the Fiesta Americana. The owner, Felipe, is a character, and loves goofing around with his customers. The Mexican food is so-

so. The Seafood is what we recommend. It's good
eating, and a great value. The plate of Lobster Tails
is our favorite item. And don't miss the house
tequila.

RESTAURANTE LE NATURA
Mexican, Health, Vegetarian, Seafood
Boulevard Kukulcan km 9.5 | Zona
Hotelera, Cancún 77500, Mexico:
52 998-883-0585
www.restaurantenatura.com
Here is a great way to start your day in the Hotel
Zone. This inexpensive little eatery is right across the

street from Señor Frog's. They have a large variety of fruit juices and smoothies they offer, including some tasty options you've probably never had. Their breakfast plates, such as the Juevos Rancheros, are big and tasty. Or if you're into healthier fare you can get the fruit platter, which is huge. And you can get your breakfast served at any time of the day, which is a feature we always like. They don't stop at breakfast. There is a good selection of tasty dishes for both vegetarians and carnivores.

THE SURFIN BURRITO
Mexican
Kukulcan Blvd. Km 9.5, Cancún, Mexico: 52-998-883-0083
https://www.facebook.com/thesurfinburrito/info?tab=overview

Absolutely the best burrito you will find in Cancún.
It's just a little hut with some counters and stools, but
it has great atmosphere. You make your selections on
an order slip, and they build it for you… Hot and
Huge. The tacos are good, but the burritos steal the
show. The smoothies are good too, and big. If you
prefer your drinks with a kick, they have a bar as
well. You might miss it, so remember it is right
across the street from Sr. Frog's next to the OXXO.
They are open 24 hours and they deliver to the hotel
zone.

LA TRANQUITA GRILL AND BAR
Pizza, Burgers, Steaks, Pastas
Ave. Kabah Mz1. Smz 13. Lote 22. Plaza Zona
Zentro, Cancún 77500, Mexico:
998-802-1841
www.latranquita.com
This little gem is located away from the tourist zone
in Cancún proper. It's a bit out of the way, so have
good directions or take a taxi. But once you've
gotten there you'll be glad you did. There is
something for everyone at La Tranquita, and it's all
good. It's better than good. Pizzas, burgers, steaks,
pastas, everything is delicious. The friendly staff
helmed by Manager Eric, who is always circulating
making sure his guests are enjoying their meal. The
space is warm and relaxing, and spotlessly clean.
Before you leave – and you won't want to leave –
have the corn cake for dessert.

TRATTORIA LA VENEZIANA DA BERTILLA
Italian, Pasta, Pizza
Tulipanes n 9 SM 22 MZ 2, Cancún 77500, Mexico:
998-884-8475
https://www.facebook.com/Trattoria-la-
venezianaCancun-Mexico-61880822973/
You can't get more authentic Italian. This is a family
run restaurant downtown. Bertilla, Luciano and
Sergio moved here from Italy five years ago, and
have been drawing devoted customers since. The
open-air dining is on a pedestrian street next to
popular Parque de las Palapas Park. The Pizzas are
real authentic Italian Pizzas… thin, thin crusts and
lots of flavor. All their pastas are perfect of course,
but we want to rave about the Gnocchi. If you ask us,
an Italian Restaurant lives or dies on its Gnocchi.
And this trattoria lives, lives, lives!

Mid-Range

BACOLI TRATORIA
Blvd. Kulkukan, Km 17. Retorno Gucumatz,
52 998 283 3800
https://hotelesemporio.com
CUISINE: Italian
DRINKS: Full Bar
SERVING: Dinner
PRICE RANGE: $$
NEIGHBORHOOD: Quintana Roo
Located in Emporio Hotel & Resort, this eatery offers
a creative menu of handmade Italian fare and pizzas
prepared in a stone oven. Favorites: Calamari and
Lasagna. Nice wine list.

ELEFANTA INDIAN CUISINE
Indian
Blvd. Kukulcan Km. 12.5 Zona Hotelera, Plaza La
Isla, Cancún 77500, Mexico: 52-998-176-8070
www.elefanta.com.mx
 Elefanta Indian is adjacent to Elefanta Thai, so
whichever is your pleasure. The ambiance is superb;
one feels transported to a bamboo paradise,
overlooking an idyllic lagoon at sunset. The food is
delicious. We love curry, and here it is made
perfectly. Be advised that the pricing structure is
such that you might feel nickel and dimed, and one is
charged extra for such things as Rice and Naan.

FRED'S HOUSE & SEAFOOD

Seafood
Kukulkan Kilometro 14.5, Across From JW Marriott
Hotel, Cancún 77500, Mexico: 52-998-840-6466
https://fredshouserestaurant.com/
This is a seafood restaurant, so have the seafood. The
kitchen perfectly prepares and presents fish. We have
many favorites here. The house Seafood Platter
features a nice assortment of their best items. Start
with the Shrimp Ceviche. The Fresh Lobster, of
course, is a feast. And we also like the octopus,
which comes drenched in butter. We're very
impressed with the kid-friendly atmosphere here.
They even have an activity room for kids, complete
with video games. And while the kids are gone, have
one of Fred's Mojitos.

LA HABICHUELA DOWNTOWN

Seafood, Steaks, Fusion

Margaritas # 25 | Parque de las
Palapas, Cancún 77500, Mexico: 52-998-884-3158
www.lahabichuela.com
Located next to beautiful Parque de la Palapas Park in
downtown Cancún, La Habichuela is a favorite with
locals and tourists alike; so we recommend you make
reservations. The Mayan décor is really well done,
and both the dining room and the garden are nice
settings, but for a romantic touch, we like the garden.
The service staff is well-trained and quite efficient.
The food is delicious. We really like the Caesar
Salad made tableside – they have lots of nice touches
like that. Their signature dish, the Cocobichuela, a
lobster and shrimp curry served in a coconut shell, is
very popular. And we recommend ending the night
with a Mayan Coffee.

LABNA

Yucatecan
Margaritas 29, Next to Parque Las Palapas,
Cancún 77500, Mexico: 52-998-892-3056
www.restaurantelabna.com/
 While in Cancún, we recommend that you get off the
beach and get to know a little of the local culture.
Labna is a quaint local place in downtown that offers
just that. The food and flavorings are that of the
Mayan and Yucatecan culture. Be prepared for
something different, and you can trust me—it's good.
The Pumpkin Seed Spread they bring out is delicious,
and we find ourselves filling up on that. But leave
room for the real food. For a nice sampling of their
dishes, get the Yucatan Trip. We highly recommend
the Lime Soup. Our favorite entrée is the Pibil

Chicken. Also high on our list is the Cactus Salad and the Chaya Drink.

LOCANDA PAOLO
Italian, Seafood, Fusion
Bonampak Avenue 145 – Corner Jurel Street, Cancún, Mexico: 52-998-887-2627
www.locandapaolo.com
Eating at Locanda Paolo is a treat we highly recommend to anyone. The whole event is a thrill for the senses. The décor is modern and trendy, but not cold. All customers are treated like VIPs by the attentive staff, led by the owner, Paolo, who is very hands-on. The menu is full of interesting and creative dishes that delight the palate. We'd like to know where they get their prosciutto from, because it is amazing. And we're always happy to find a restaurant that makes a good authentic Cream Puff!

MAKI TACO
Blvd. Kukulcan, 52 998 848 7500
https://oasishoteles.com/en/restaurants/maki-taco
CUISINE: Mexican/Japanese/Sushi
DRINKS: Full Bar
SERVING: Dinner, Closed Mon & Tues.
PRICE RANGE: $$$
NEIGHBORHOOD: Quintana Roo
Upscale hotel eatery offering a creative menu of a variety of cuisines. Excellent sushi. Favorites: Beef teriyaki and Cold calamari with mole sauce. Impressive tequila selection.

SAVIO'S BISTRO BY LA DOLCE

Italian
km 15 Zona Hotelera | Across from the Gran Meliá
Hotel, Cancún, Mexico:
52-998-884-3393
www.cancunitalianrestaurant.com
Located in the Hotel Zone, Savio's is the kind of
place you try once, and then you eat there several
times a week. The ambience is relaxed with dining
indoors and out. The staff is friendly and efficient.
All their food is consistently high quality and
delicious. We will name a few of our favorites:
Eggplant Parmesan, Veal Scallopini, Lasagna

Bollognaise, Calamari. The kitchen accommodates special needs and requests.

Pricey

BLACK HOLE
Grand Oasis Sens Blvd. Kukulkan Km 19.5,
52 998 891 5000
https://oasishoteles.com/es/restaurantes/black-hole
CUISINE: International
DRINKS: Full Bar
SERVING: Dinner, Closed Sundays
PRICE RANGE: $$$$
NEIGHBORHOOD: Quintana Roo
Located at The Pyramid at Grand Oasis, this eatery offers a unique dining experience. Food is served amongst performances. This is a 20+ course meal. Note: it is so dark the hosts have to guide you to your table. After you eat each course, they'll ask you to guess what it as—it's so dark you won't be able to see it, as a rule. But a fun evening. (Don't trip!)

CHIC CABARET & RESTAURANT COSTA MUJERES
Boulevard Vialidad Paseo Mujeres Sm 3 MZ 1 Lt 10, 52 998 868 5200
https://www.palladiumhotelgroup.com
CUISINE: Dinner Theater
DRINKS: Full Bar
SERVING: Dinner, Closed Mon & Tues.
PRICE RANGE: $$$$

NEIGHBORHOOD: Quintana Roo

Located in the palladium resort/TRS hotel, Chic Cabaret offers an energetic dinner show fusing dance, music and gastronomy, all in a dimly lit romantic room. The 7-course meal and drinks (which never stop coming) are all included in one price. Reservations recommended, as space is limited. Plan on a longish evening, starting at 7:30 or so and lasting till 11. With the dinner and the show, it stretches out.

DU MEXIQUE

French

Av. Bonampak 109, esq. calle Pargo, Mz. 17, Sm. 3, Centro, Cancún, Mexico: 52-998-884-5889

www.dumexique.com/

This is one of the most unique and extraordinary dining experiences we have encountered. Du Mexique is the labor of love of Chef and Owner Alain Grimond, a master of his craft. Inside an elegant

gallery of contemporary art you will be courteously
seated and given what could be the meal of your life.
Don't touch the menu, which changes every day. Let
Chef Grimond work his magic and choose for you a
meal that you will remember forever. We are
effusive in our praise, but we do not exaggerate.
Guests have been moved to tears by their experience
here. When your meal is over… when you have
wiped the last bit ambrosia off the dessert plate and
sucked it from your finger in reverent gratitude …
have the coffee.

HARRY'S PRIME STEAKHOUSE AND RAW BAR

Steak, Shellfish
Blvd. Kukulcan Km. 14.2,
No.1, Cancún 17520, Mexico: 52-998-840-6550
www.harrys.com.mx
Harry's is on par with any steakhouse you'll find in
the US. They serve only imported Prime USDA or
Kobe beef. The service is superb. The interior of the
restaurant is simply stunning. The raw bar also offers
an excellent selection of oysters. When you have had
your fill, fill up a little more on dessert, of which our
favorite is the Key Lime Pie. Their signature touch is
a complimentary portion of Cotton Candy after the
meal, which we find amusing.

L'ESCARGOT

French
Calle Pina #27, SM-25 | Quintana Roo
77500, Cancún, Mexico: 52-998-887-6337
http://lescargot.restaurantwebexperts.com/

Situated in a renovated house near downtown Cancún, a mother and daughter team have created a delicious haven for food lovers. The ambience is cozy and warm, and the women give wonderful service. The food is delightful. There is an endless supply of delicious homemade bread. Our favorite dishes include the French Onion Soup and the Lamb. We also love their Patés.

LA PALAPA BELGA

European, International
Calle Quetzal No 13, Hotel Imperial
Laguna, Cancún 77500, Mexico:
52 998-883-5454
www.lapalapabelga.com
La Palapa Belga is the archetypal "hidden gem," located at the back of the Hotel Imperial Laguna. It can be a bit of a challenge to find, so we recommend taking a taxi. Once found, though you will be glad of the effort. The minimalist and rustic open-air

restaurant is uniquely situated on the mainland side of lagoon, with a breathtaking view of the Hotel Zone across the water. The food here is consistently high class. Only the best of restaurants can carry off a Duck Breast as well as here. We also recommend you indulge in the decadent Escargot. Our top pick for dessert… the Belgian Chocolate Mousse.

RESTAURANTE BENAZUZA
Blvd. Kukulcan Km 19.5, 52 998 891 500
https://oasishoteles.com/es/restaurantes/benazuza
CUISINE: Mexican
DRINKS: Full Bar
SERVING: Dinner, Closed Sunday
PRICE RANGE: $$$$
NEIGHBORHOOD: Quintana Roo
Located downstairs in the Grand Oasis Sens Hotel, this upscale eatery offers a creative menu with a strong Mexican influence. First stop is the bar, where

you get 5 creative cocktails then you're taken to your table. This is a 20-course meal ending in 3 sets of desserts. Favorites: Sea Bass and Pink Mole Duck.

RESTAURANTE CAREYES

Blvd. Kukulcan Km. 16.5, 52 998 881 7000
www.grandoasiscancunresort.com
CUISINE: Seafood/Mexican/Steakhouse
DRINKS: Full Bar
SERVING: Lunch & Dinner, Closed Thursday
PRICE RANGE: $$$$
NEIGHBORHOOD: Quintana Roo
Elegant eatery serves traditional Mexican fare with a French twist. Favorites: Bacon Filet served with a side of oyster Rockefeller and Shrimp & Fish ceviche. Dress code.

RESTAURANTE CHIANTI
HOTEL NYX CANCUN

Blvd. Kukulkan Manzana 52 Km. 11.5, 52 998 848 9300
www.chiantirestaurant.net/dine-in.html
CUISINE: Italian
DRINKS: Full Bar
SERVING: Dinner, Closed Tuesdays
PRICE RANGE: $$$$
NEIGHBORHOOD: Quintana Roo
Upscale eatery offering a creative menu of authentic Italian fare. Vegetarian options. Favorites: Pollo & Gamberoni Alla Griglia (Large boneless breast of chicken and large Gulf shrimp) and Ribeye Steak topped with rich cream sauce with shallots and green peppercorns. Excellent wine selection.

RESTAURANTE UMAMI
HOTEL NYX
Boulevard Kukulkan K.m. 11.5 Interior,
52 998 848 9300
www.nyxhotels.com
CUISINE: Japanese/Sushi
DRINKS: Full Bar
SERVING: Dinner
PRICE RANGE: $$$
NEIGHBORHOOD: Quintana Roo
Modern designed eatery offering incredible ocean
views. Great sushi. Favorites: Miso soup and
Sashimi. Creative cocktails.

SASI
Thai cuisine
CasaMagna Marriott Cancun Resort, Boulevard
Kukulcan, Retorno Chac L-41,
Cancún 77500, Mexico: 52-998-881-2000
www.sasi-thai.com
Sasi Thai is located on the grounds of the Casa
Magna Marriott. It has a wonderful ambience with
seating in thatched cubicles. The service is friendly
and efficient. They have the dishes you would expect
from a Thai restaurant, and we really enjoy the Pad
Thai. The Duck Curry is also quite tasty. We were
also quite charmed with the Chocolate Tamarind
Dessert.

TORA MEXICO
Blvd. Kukulcan Km. 15, 52 998 313 4128
www.toramexico.com